For Elma Otto Westney

Text copyright © 1988 by Harriet Ziefert.
Illustrations copyright © 1988 by Mavis Smith.
All rights reserved.
Published by Bantam Books, Inc.
Published simultaneously in United States and Canada.
Printed in Singapore for Harriet Ziefert, Inc.
ISBN: 0-553-05454-6

WHAT DO I TOUCH?

HARRIET ZIEFERT
AND
MAVIS SMITH

BANTAM BOOKS
TORONTO · NEW YORK · LONDON · SYDNEY · AUCKLAND

I like the softness
of snow
on a cold winter's day.

I like the wetness
of water
on a hot summer's day.

Mud feels squishy
between my fingers.

Sand feels tickly
between my toes.

A cat's fur
is soft and silky
to my touch.

A frog's skin
is bumpy, lumpy!
And cool, too.

Touch a rosebush—
it feels prickly!

I don't touch HOT.
I don't touch SHARP.

Once I nearly touched a butterfly,
but as my hand came near,
it just flew away!

WHAT DO YOU THINK:

What is the softest thing you've ever touched?

The squishiest?   The hardest

The bumpiest?   The scratchiest?

The warmest?   The coolest?